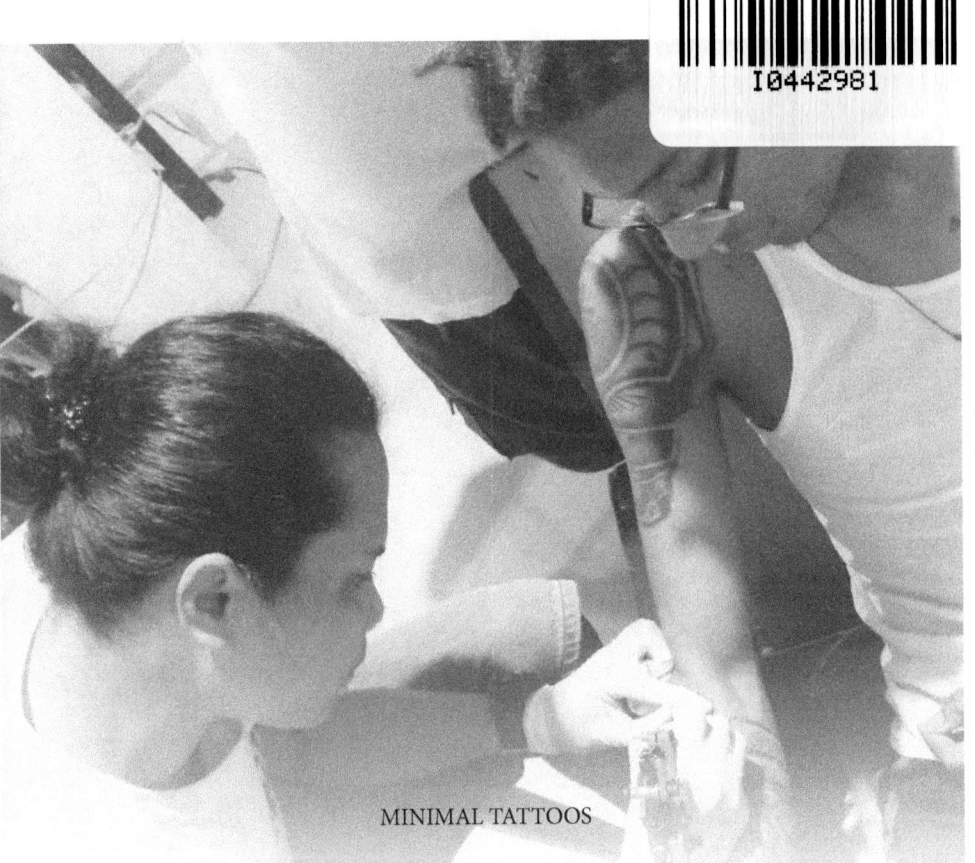

MINIMAL TATTOOS

This is a modern book of trending and meaningful minimal, small or flash tattoo design symbols in the tattoo world. A perfect reference book for Tattoo beginners or even for Professional Tattoo Artists. All design content are drawn or illustrated and categorized properly so that you will effortlessly find what type of design you are looking for during your tattoo session, study or practice.

Here are some list of the remarkable designs:

Geometric Designs

Traditional design

Symbols / Magical / Runes / Zodiac Signs

Animals / Eagles / Reptiles / Bear / Tiger / Birds

Bodies / Eyes / Hands / Pinup

Landscape / Waves / Plants / Flowers / Leaves

Cool Stuffs / Shoes / Cigarette / Cards / Games / Foods

Musical / Instruments / Notes

Skulls / Butterflies / Stones

Arrows / Ornamental

All rights reserved.

No part of this book may be reproduced, distributed or transmitted in any form or by any means, including recording, photocopying, or other electronic methods, without the prior written permission of the publisher.

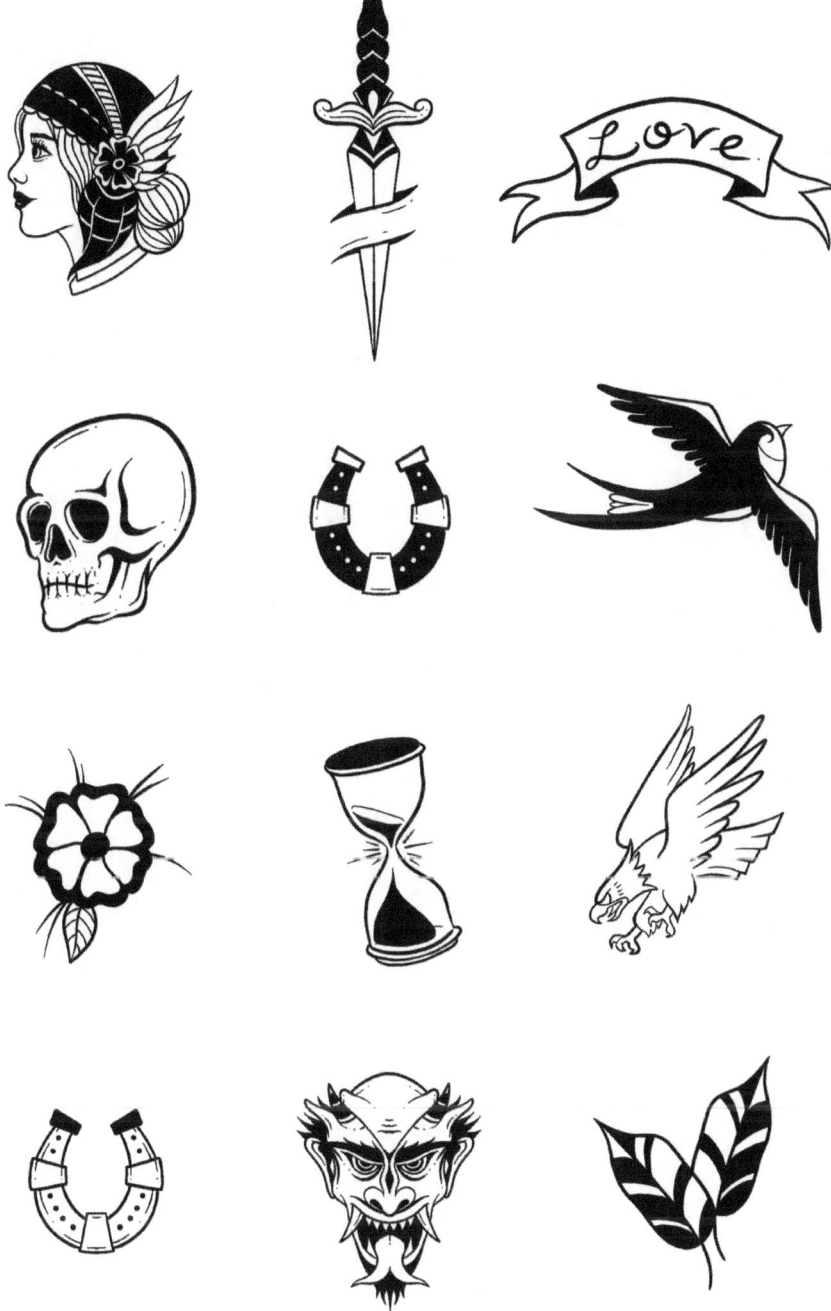

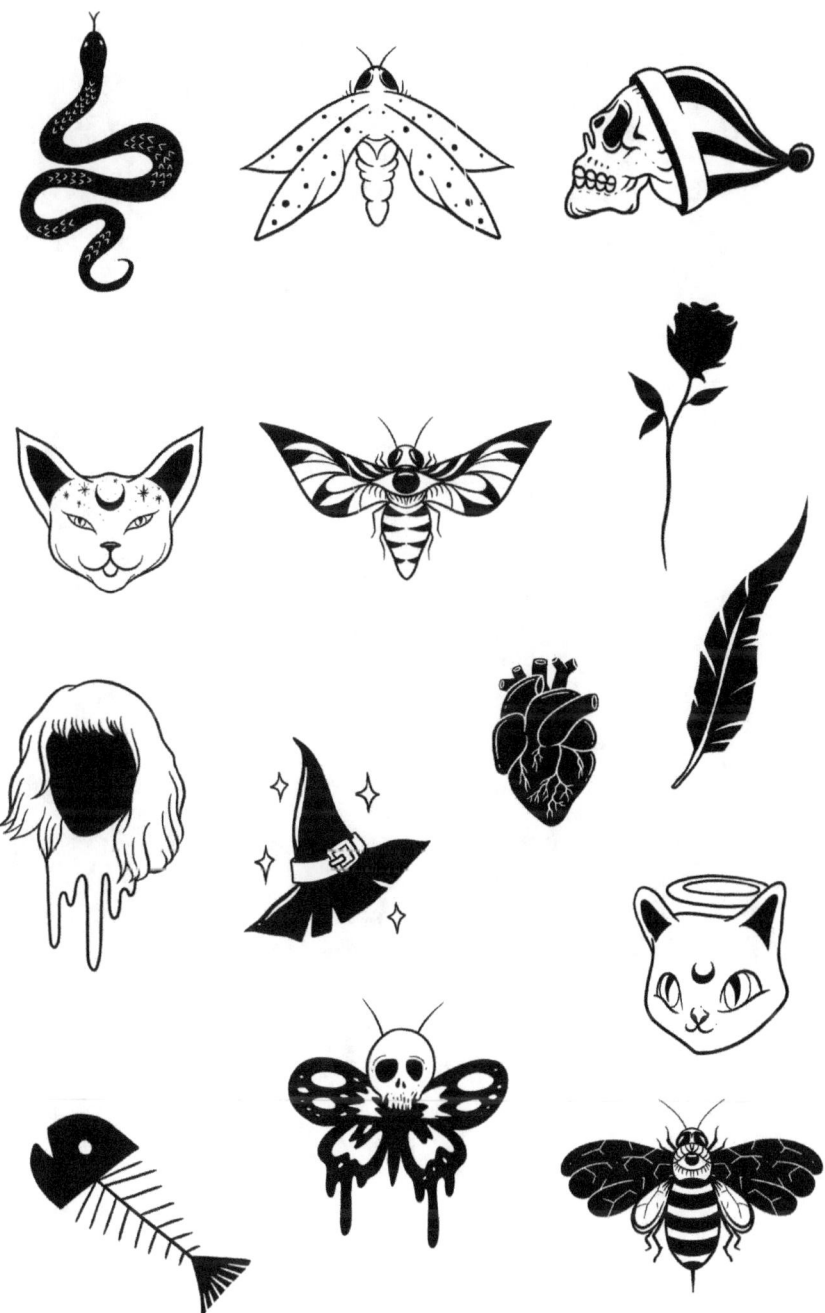

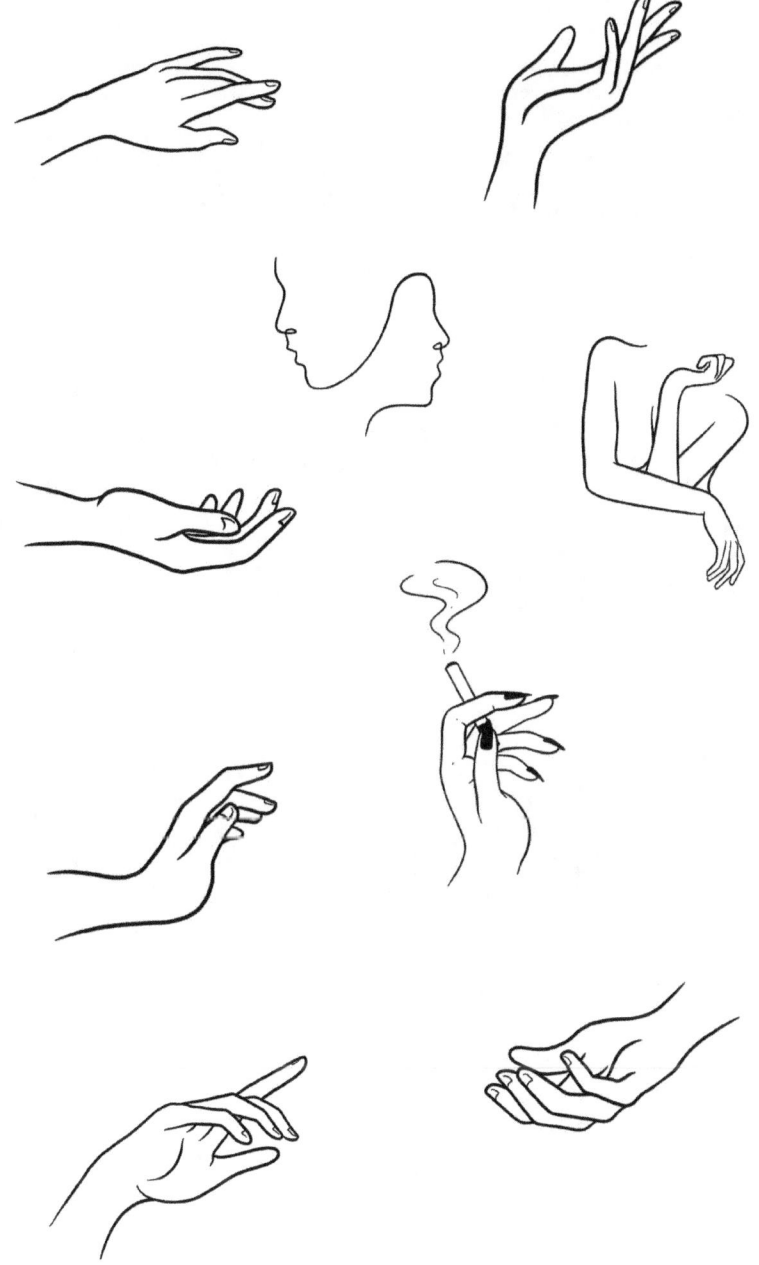

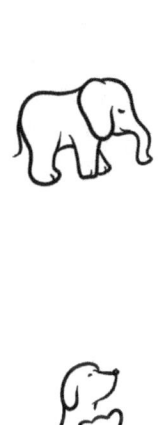
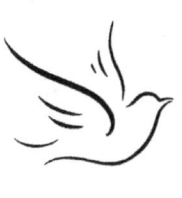
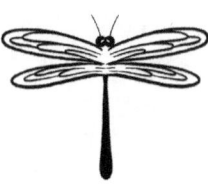
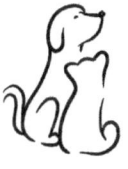

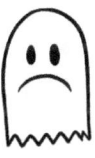

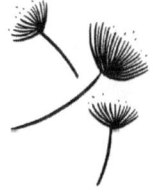

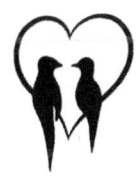
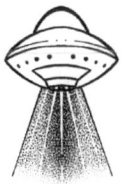
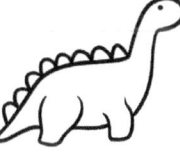

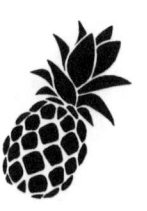

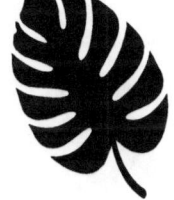

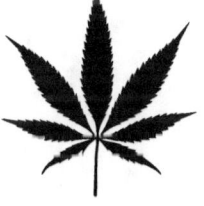
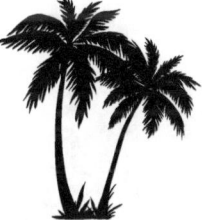
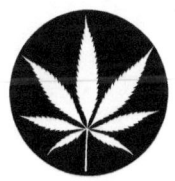

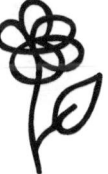

 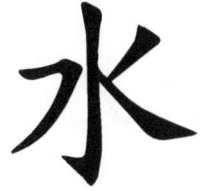 

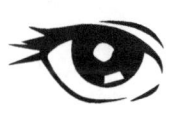 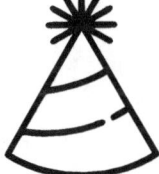 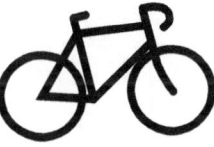

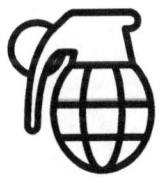 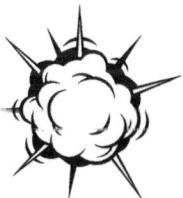 

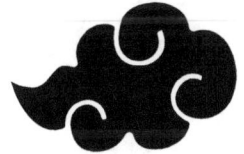 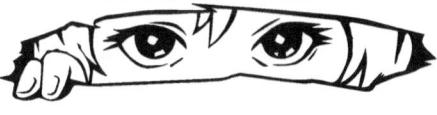

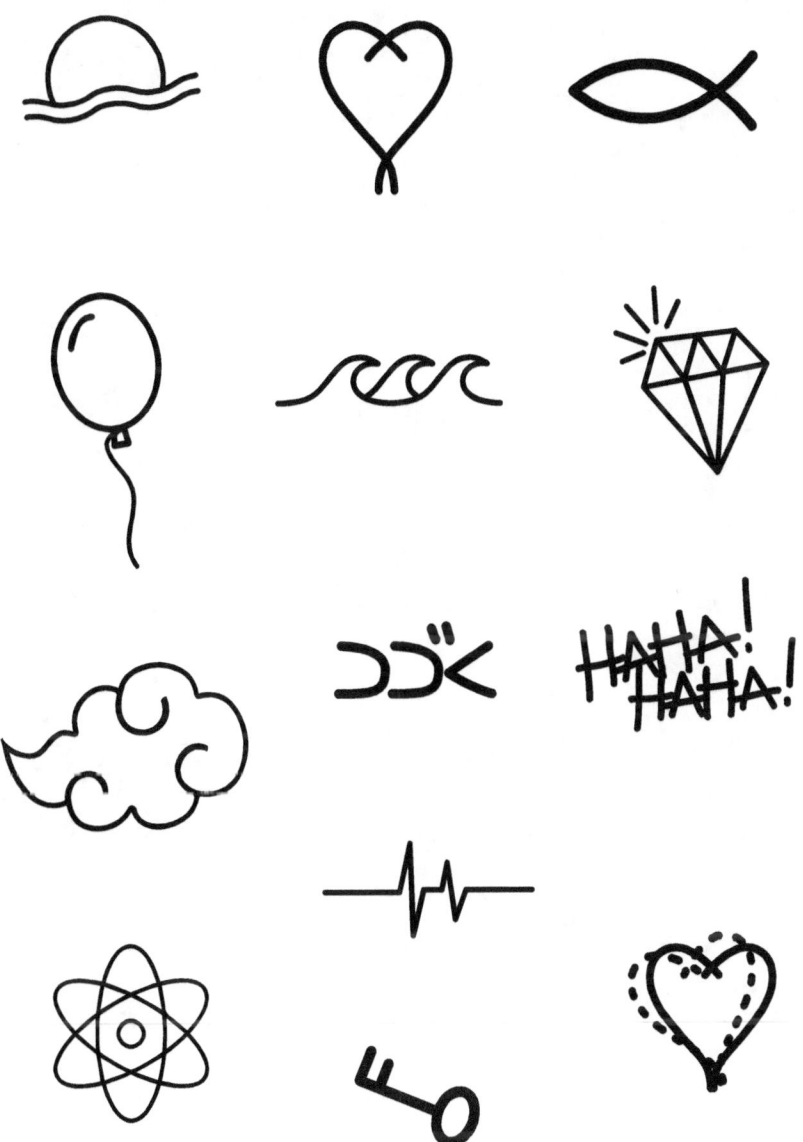

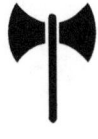

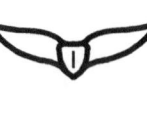

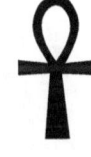
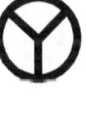
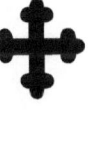
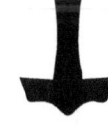
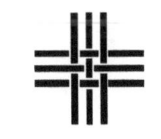

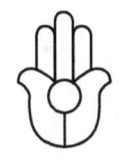 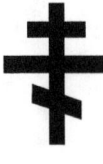 

 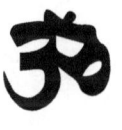 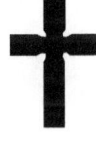

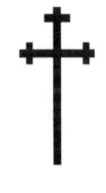 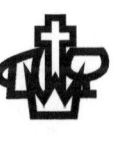 

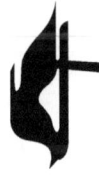 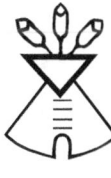 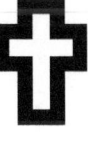

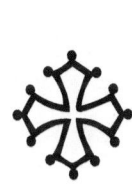  

 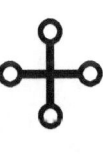 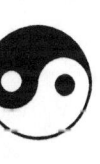

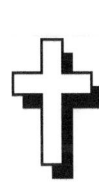 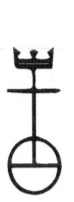 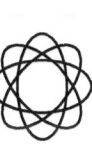

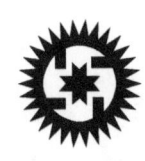
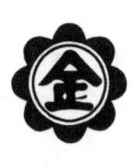

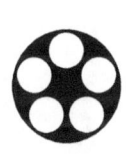
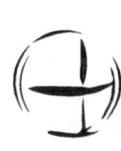

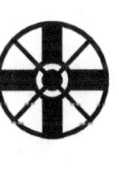
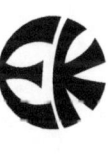

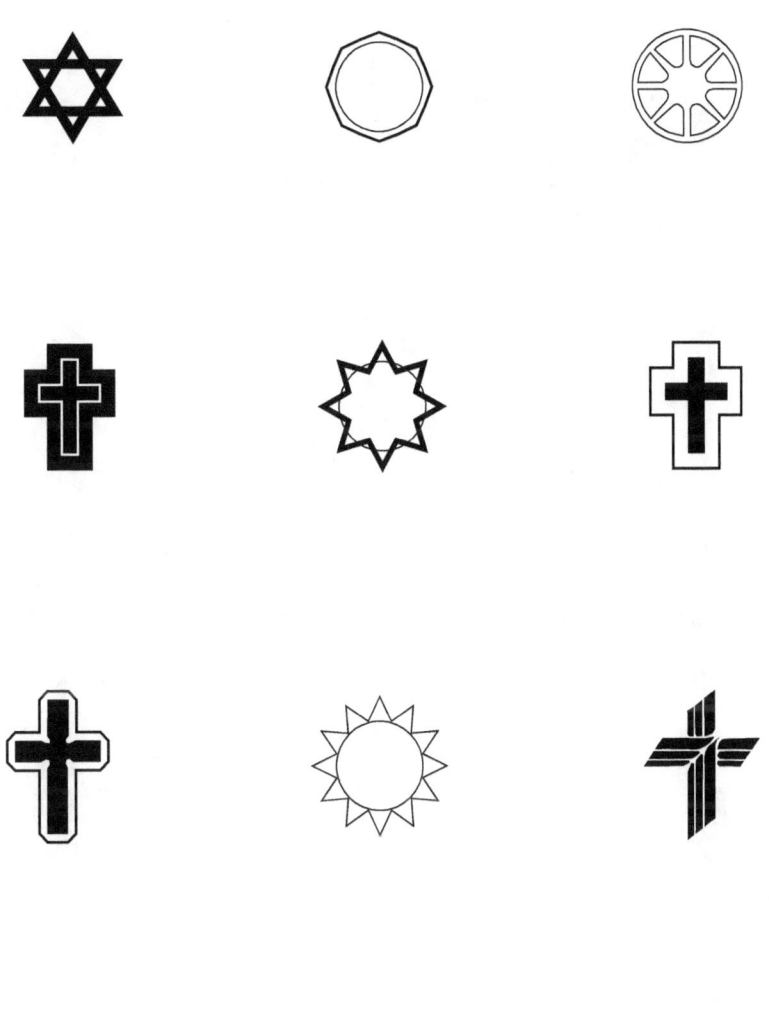

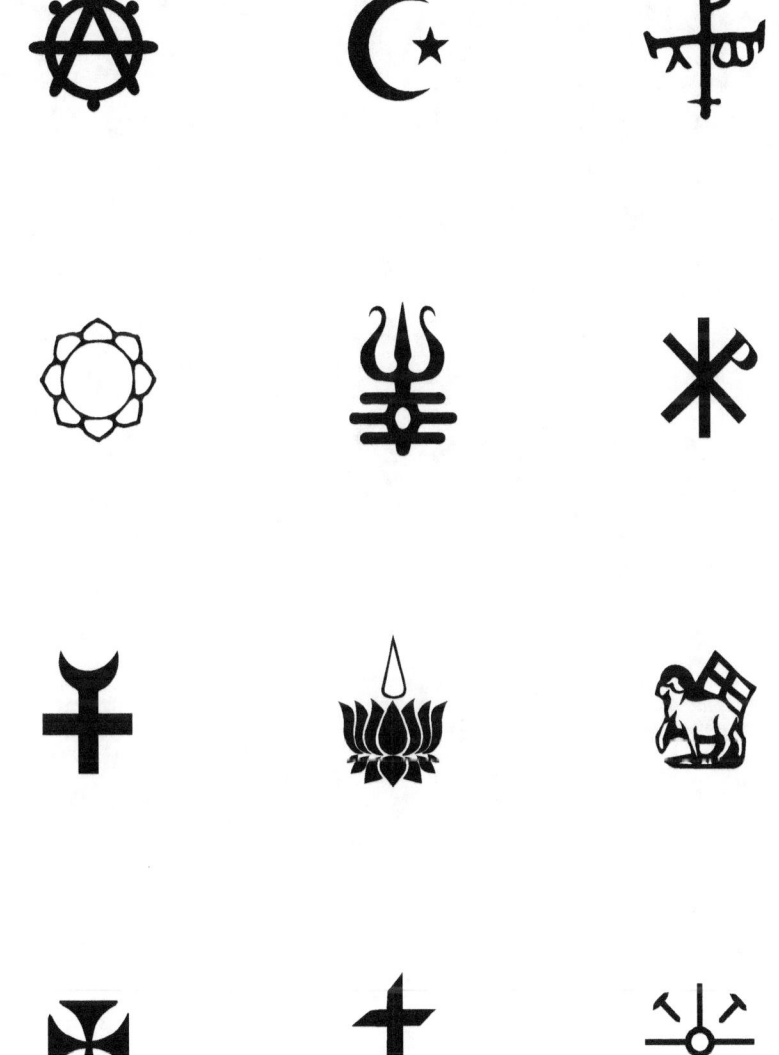

Angelic Zibu Symbols

Abu: Sacred Unity

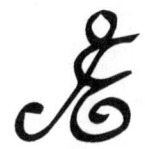
Akunate: Centeredness

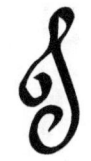
Ani: Nurture Yourself

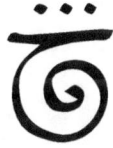
Atu: Persistence

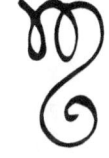
Atuna: Release Expectations

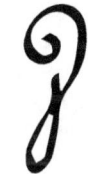
Anoko: Patience

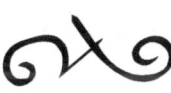
Anona: Fortitude

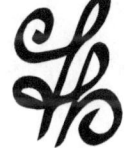
Anu: Gratitude

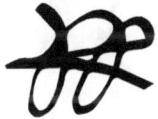
Arani: Beauty

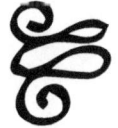
Asi: Authenticity

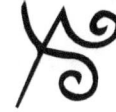
Awanda: Encouragement

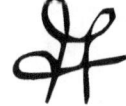
Habukana: Effortless Connection

Hamada: Vitality

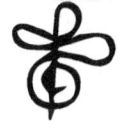
Hana: Peacekeeper

Hatumi: Acceptance of Optimum Health

  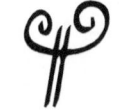 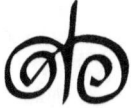

| Hazu: Kindness | Huka: Awakening | Imono: Creativity | Imu: Divine Essense |

 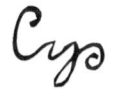 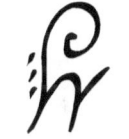 

| Kalu: SynthesisK | unata: Nature | Lahika: AbundanceM | atanu: Receptivity |

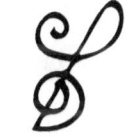  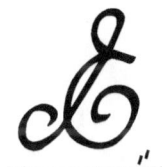 

| Nakata: Heart Song | Rasini: Embrace Life | Rikumana: Listen Within | Sati: Beacon of Hope |

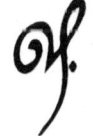  

| Shikawa: Sacred PlaceS | okana: TransitionT | akama: ReciprocityT | ama: Friendship |

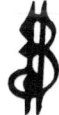   

| Tatama: Order out of Chaos | Tatina: Willingness | Tina: Thrive Present Mpment | Ziwa: Universal Love |

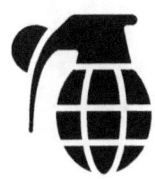 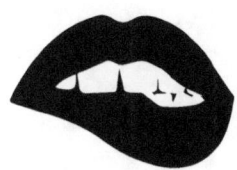 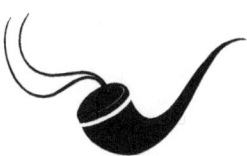
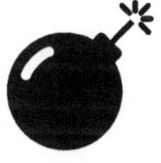 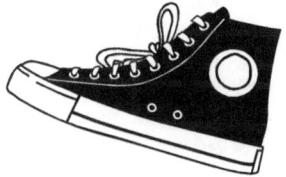 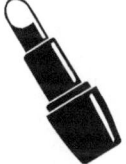
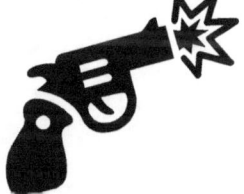  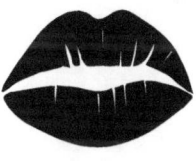
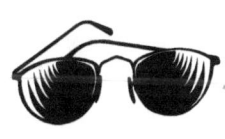 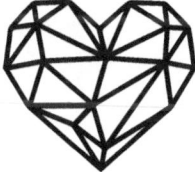 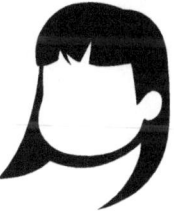

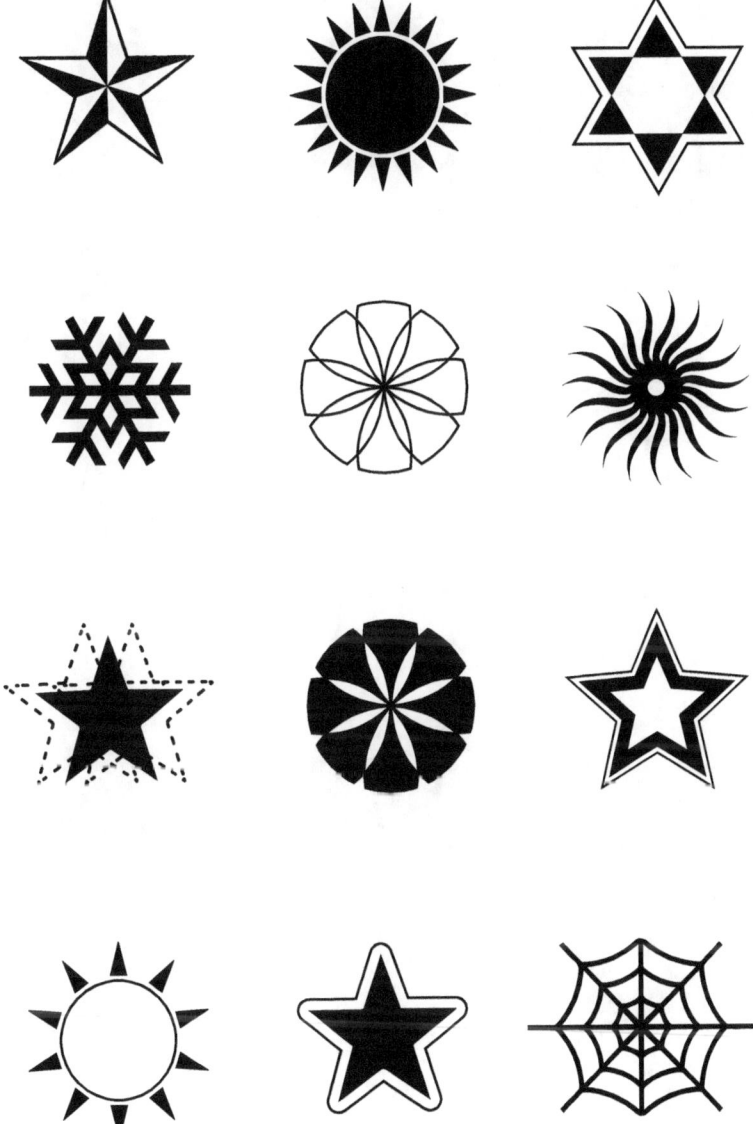

ZODIAC SIGN SYMBOLS

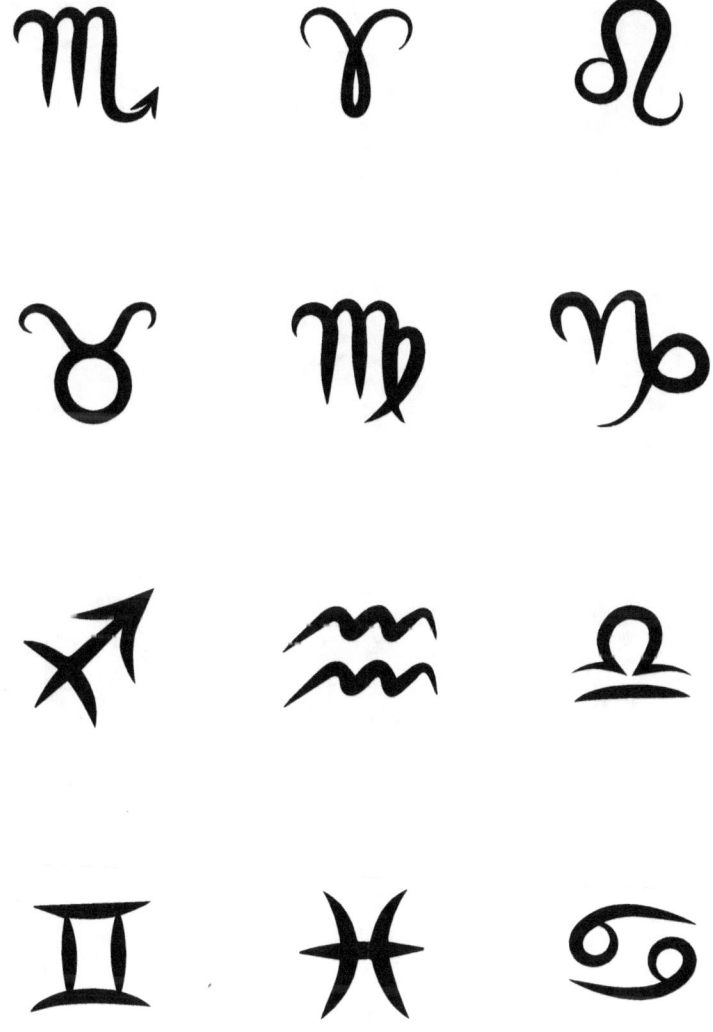

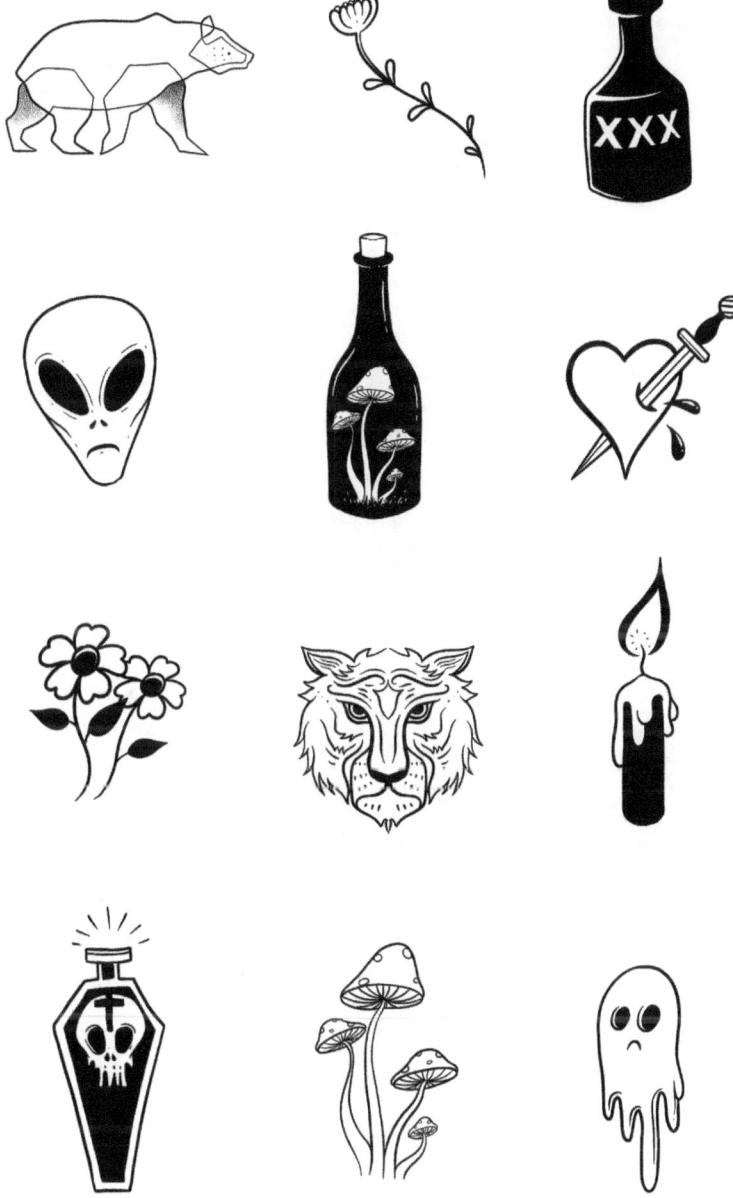

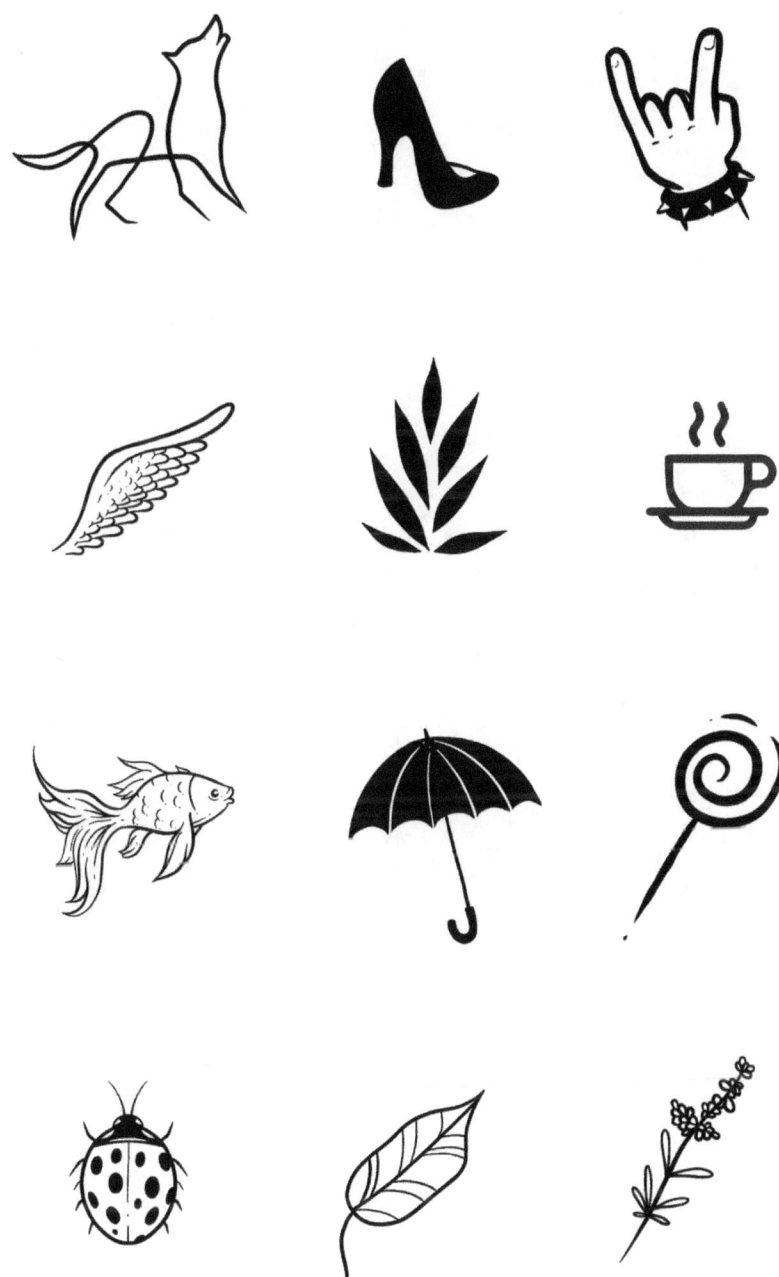

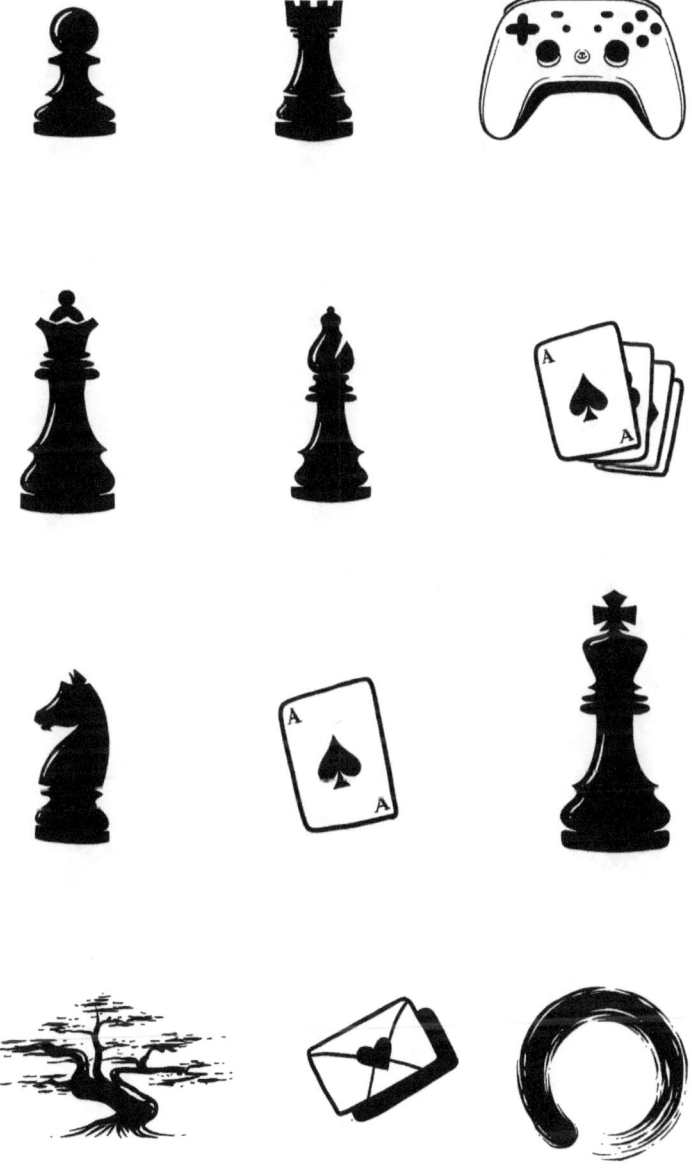

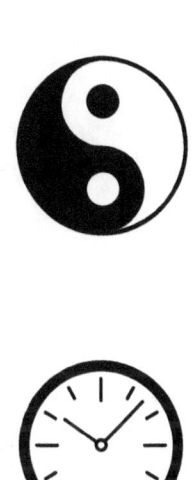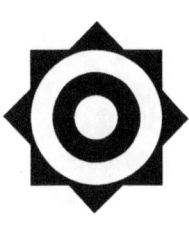
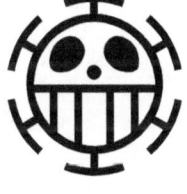
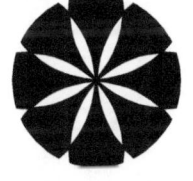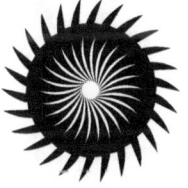
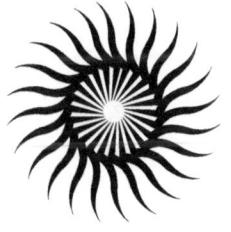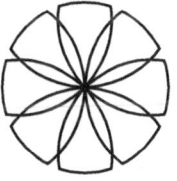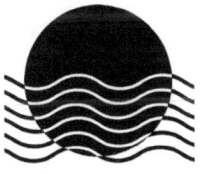

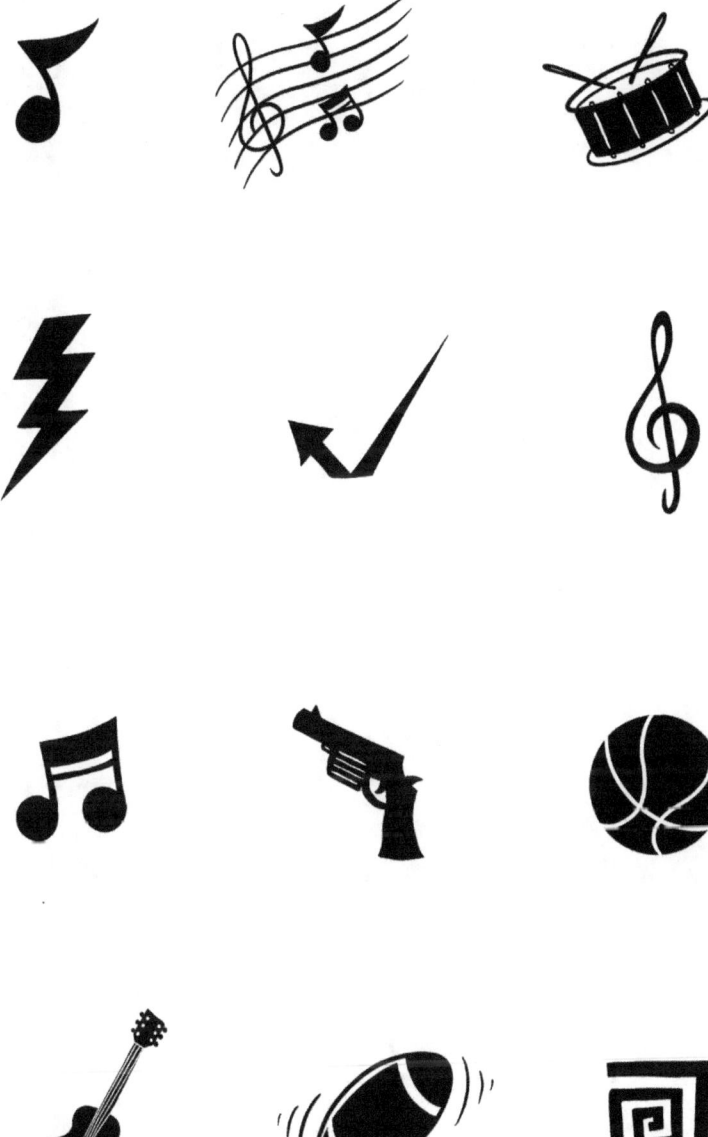

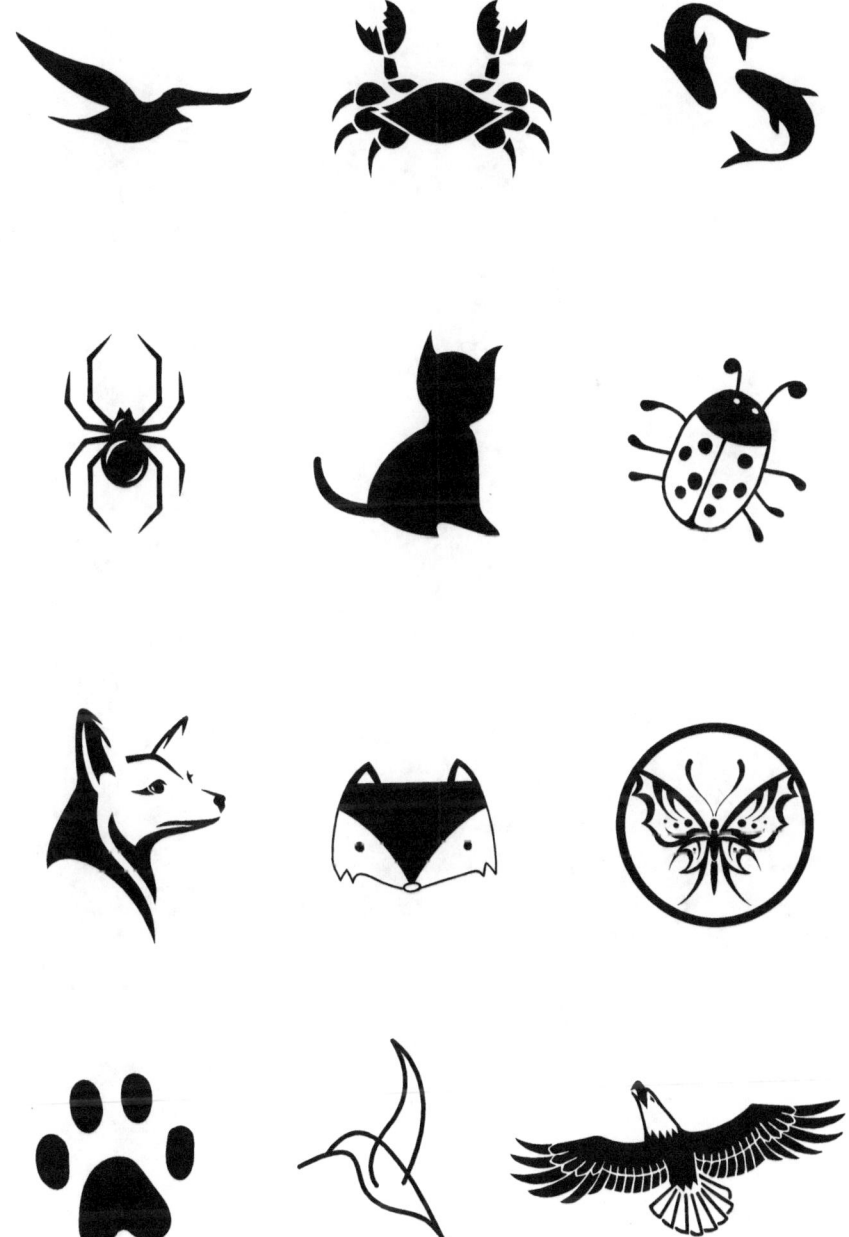

ᚠᚢᚦᚨᚱᚲ

ᚷᚹᚺᚾᛁᛉ

ᛃᛈᛇᛉᛋᛏᛒ

ᛖᛗᛚᛠᛜᛝ

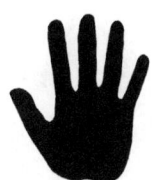

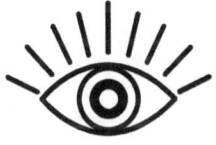
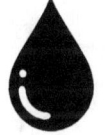
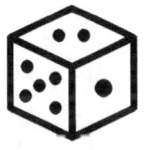
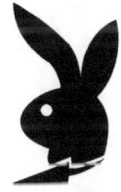

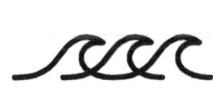
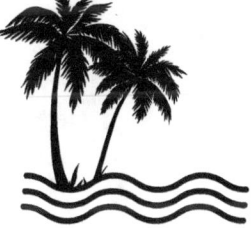

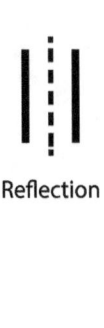
Reflection

Decay

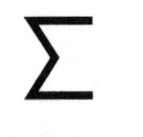
Indeterminacy

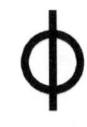
Sculpture

Landscape

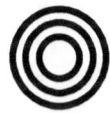
Haptic

Movement

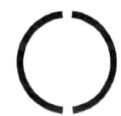
Collaboration

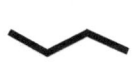
Time

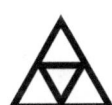
Geometry

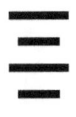
Memory

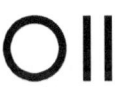
Video

Hidden unknown

Texture

Drawing

Art

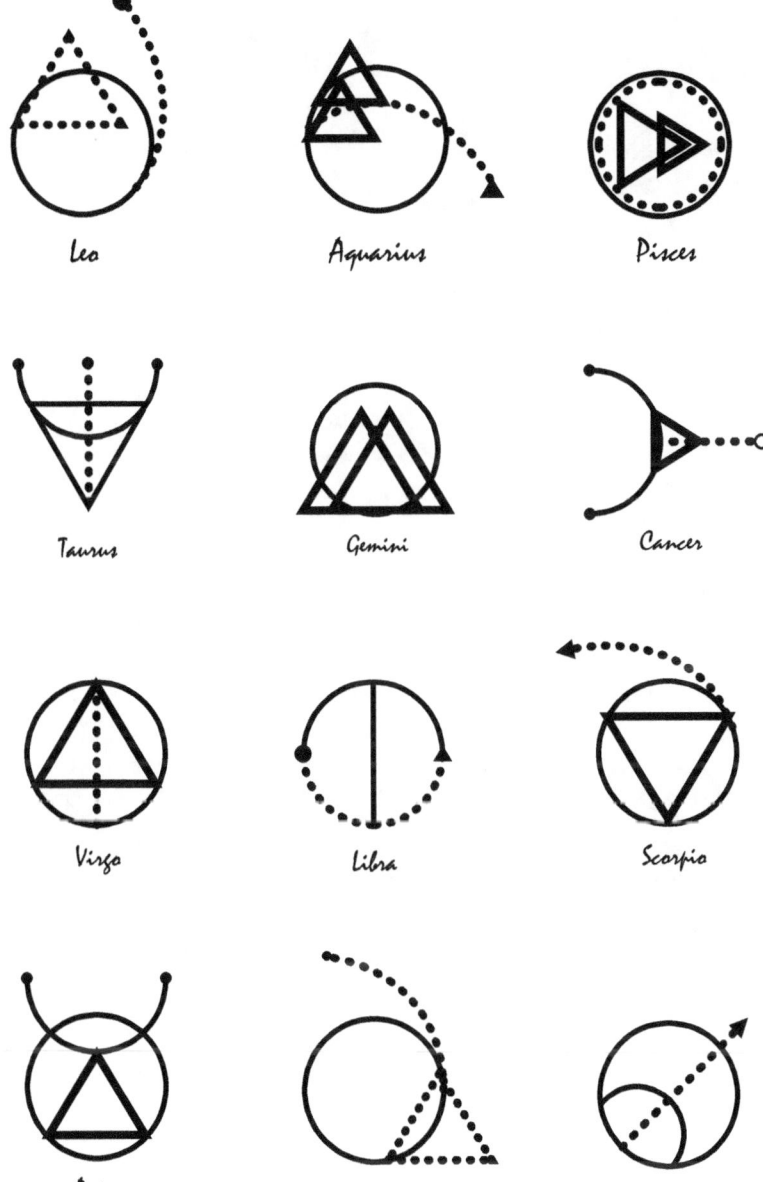

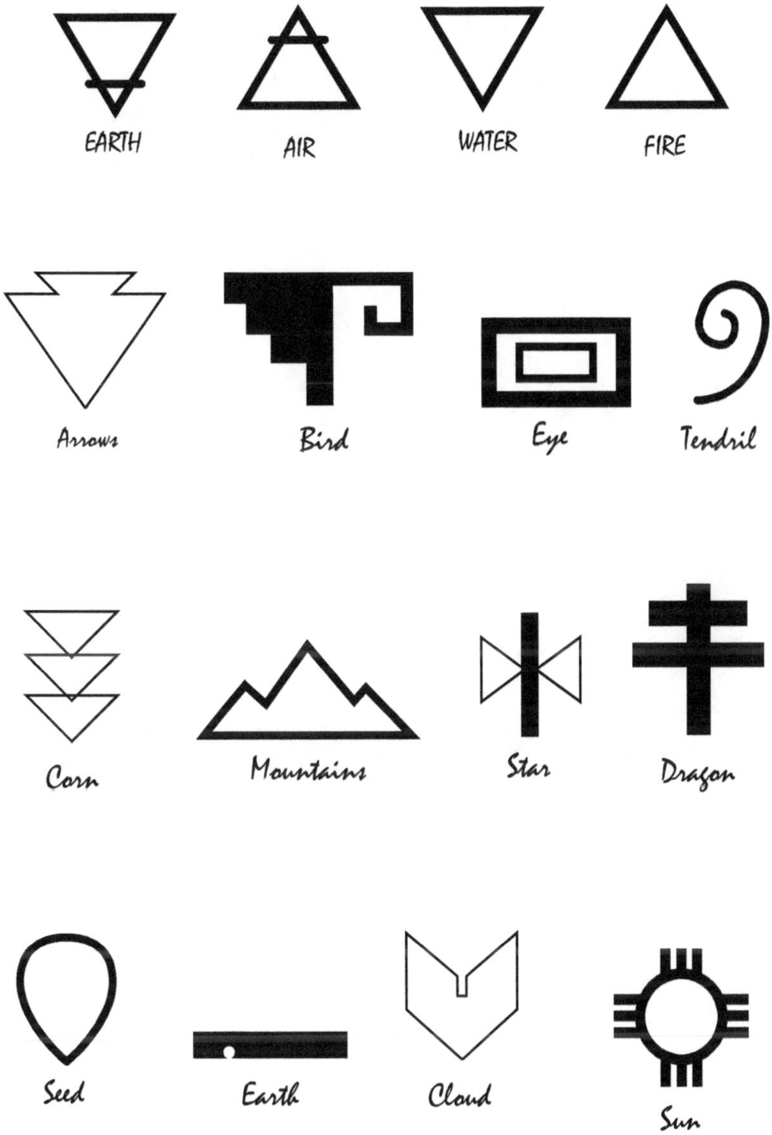

EARTH   AIR   WATER   FIRE

Arrows   Bird   Eye   Tendril

Corn   Mountains   Star   Dragon

Seed   Earth   Cloud   Sun

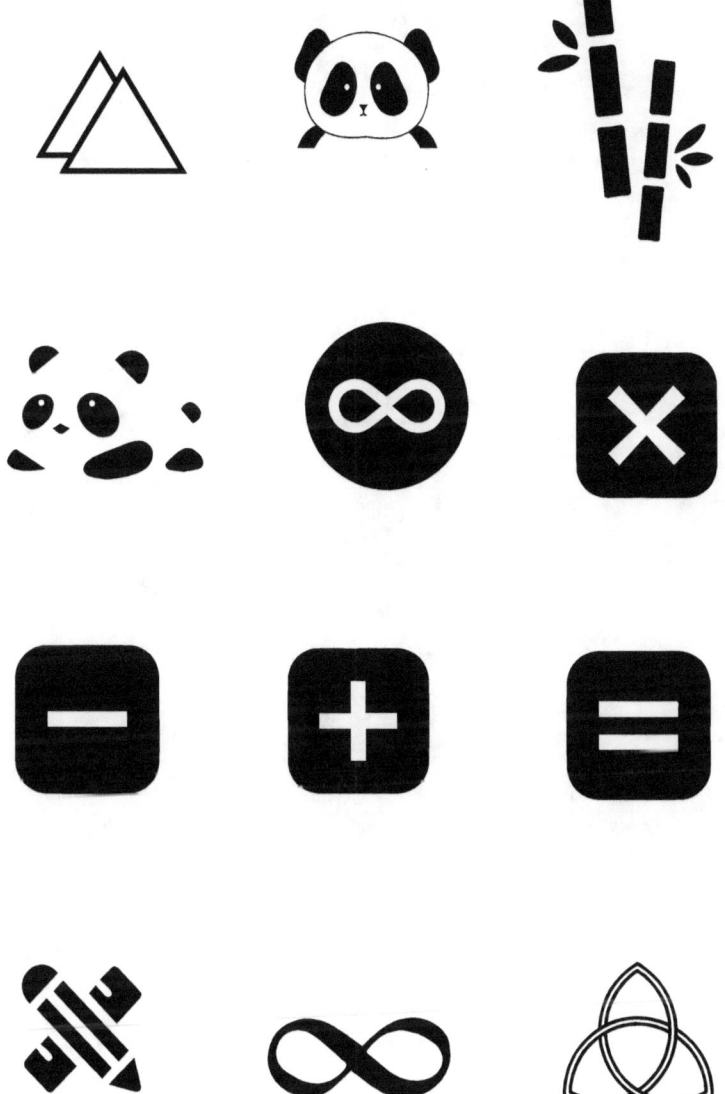

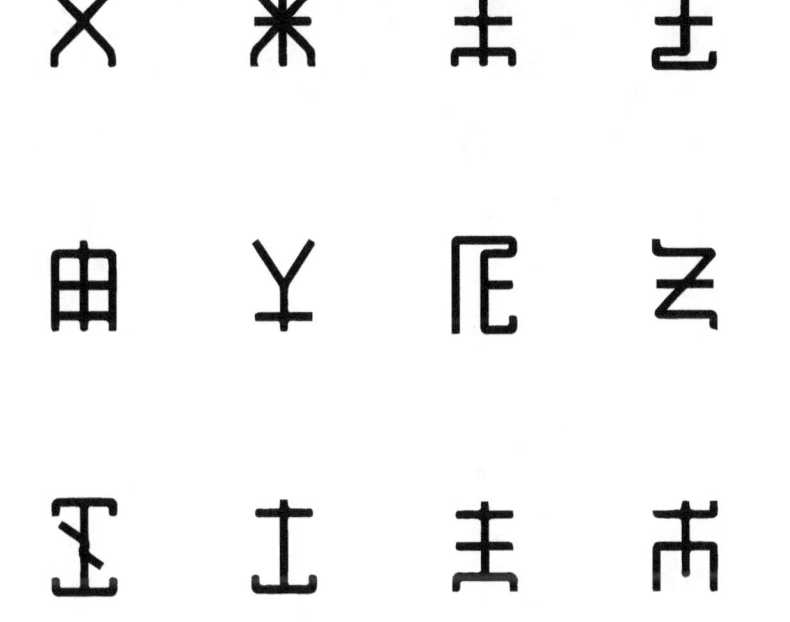

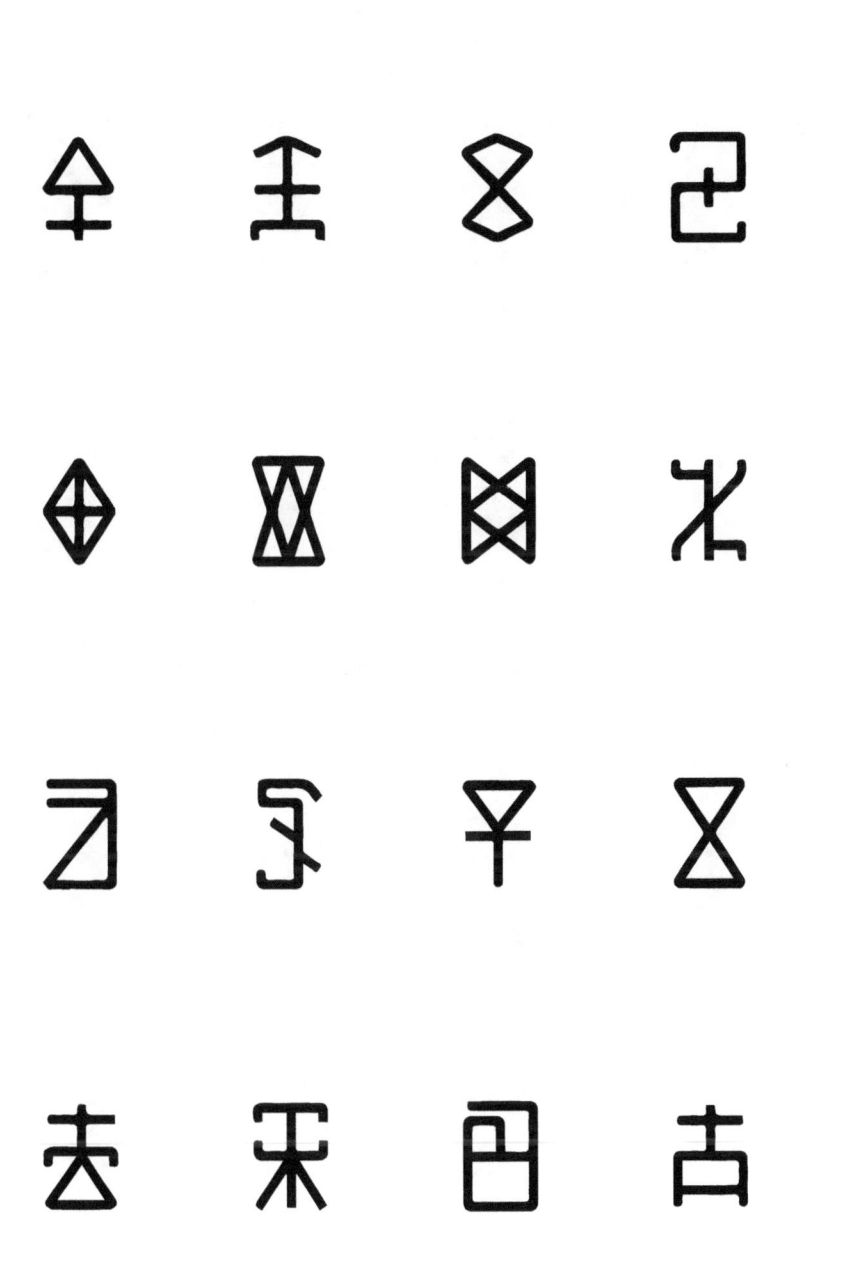

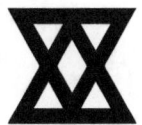
CONNECT

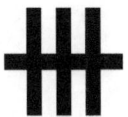
FRIENDS

UNDERSTAND

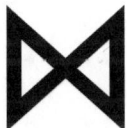
REFLECT

TRANSCEND

CHALLENGE

POWER

EXPRESS

COMBINE

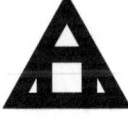
HOME

EXPLORE

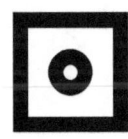
TRUTH

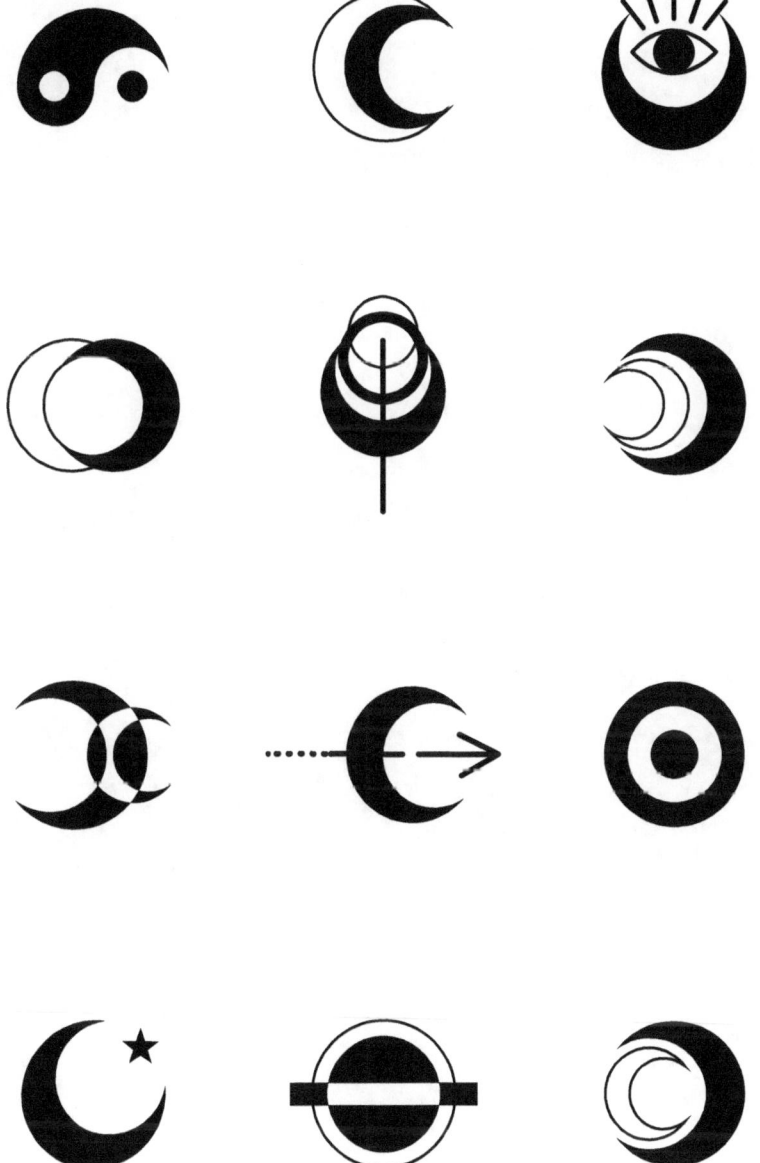

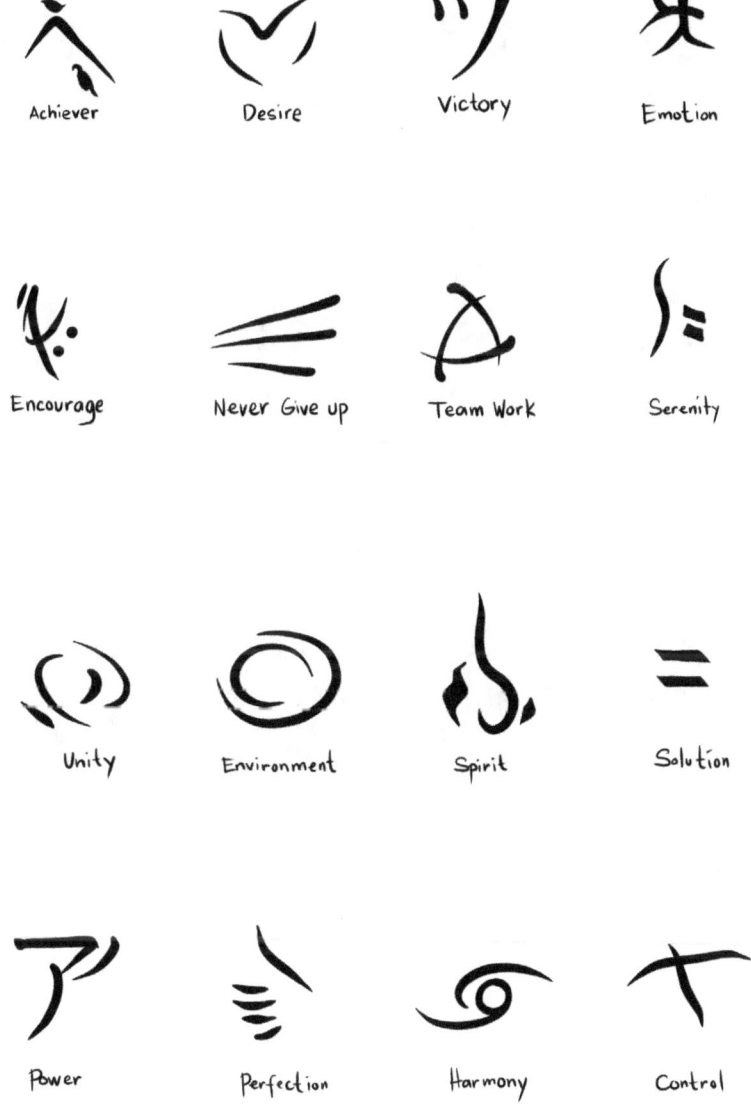

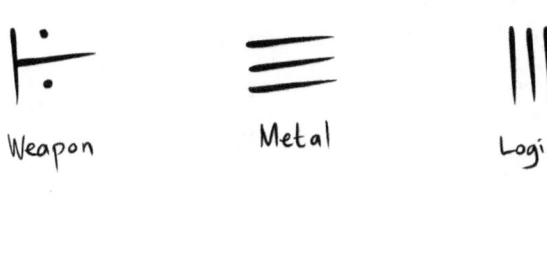

Weapon Metal Logic

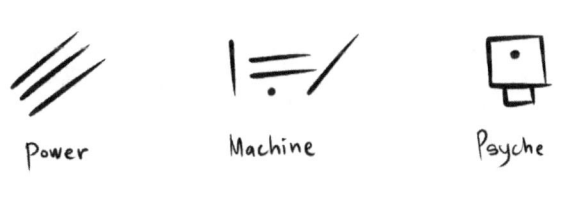

Power Machine Psyche

City Imagination Safety

Relationship

Magical Symbols of the Elves of Fyn

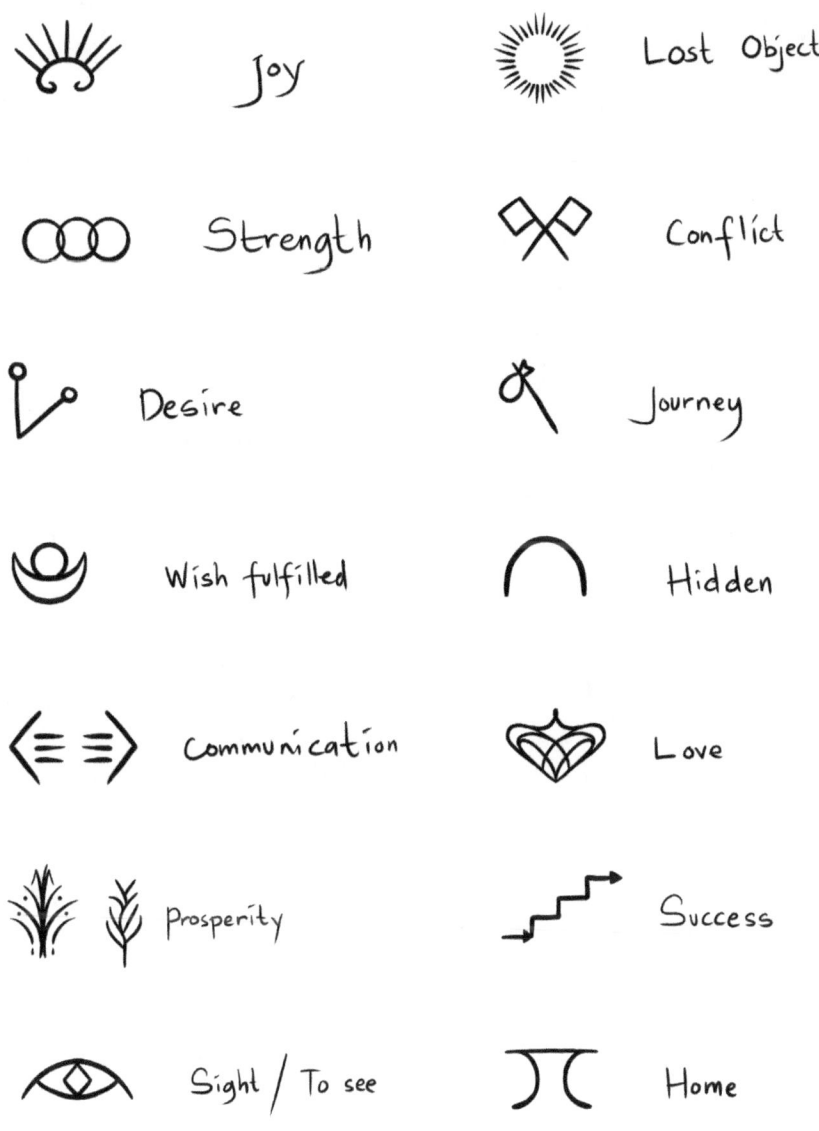

◊·◊	Ward / Protection
⊙	Lustra / The World
☼	Science / Atom
?	Spirit / Diaphon
(glyph)	The Rikku / Bird Ferin
¡○¡	Ocean / River
ʎ	Harvest / Earth
⚡	Honor
\·/	War / Fire
⚇	Lagom
·ʋʋ	Realm / Plane
·ß·	Ferin

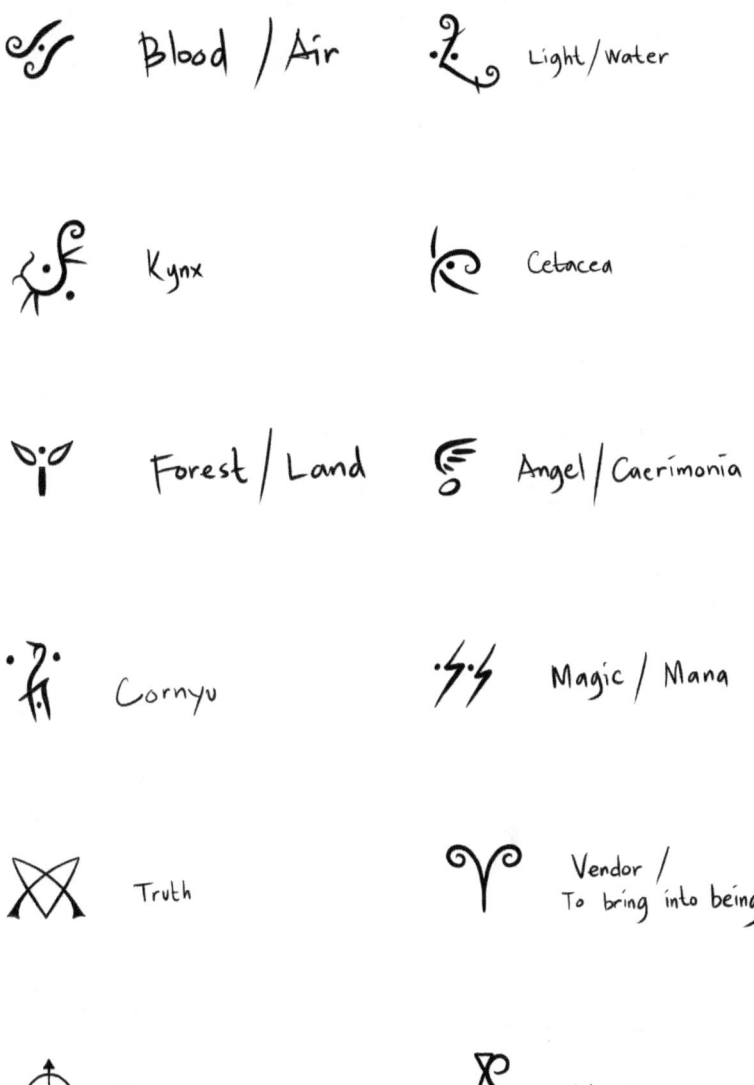

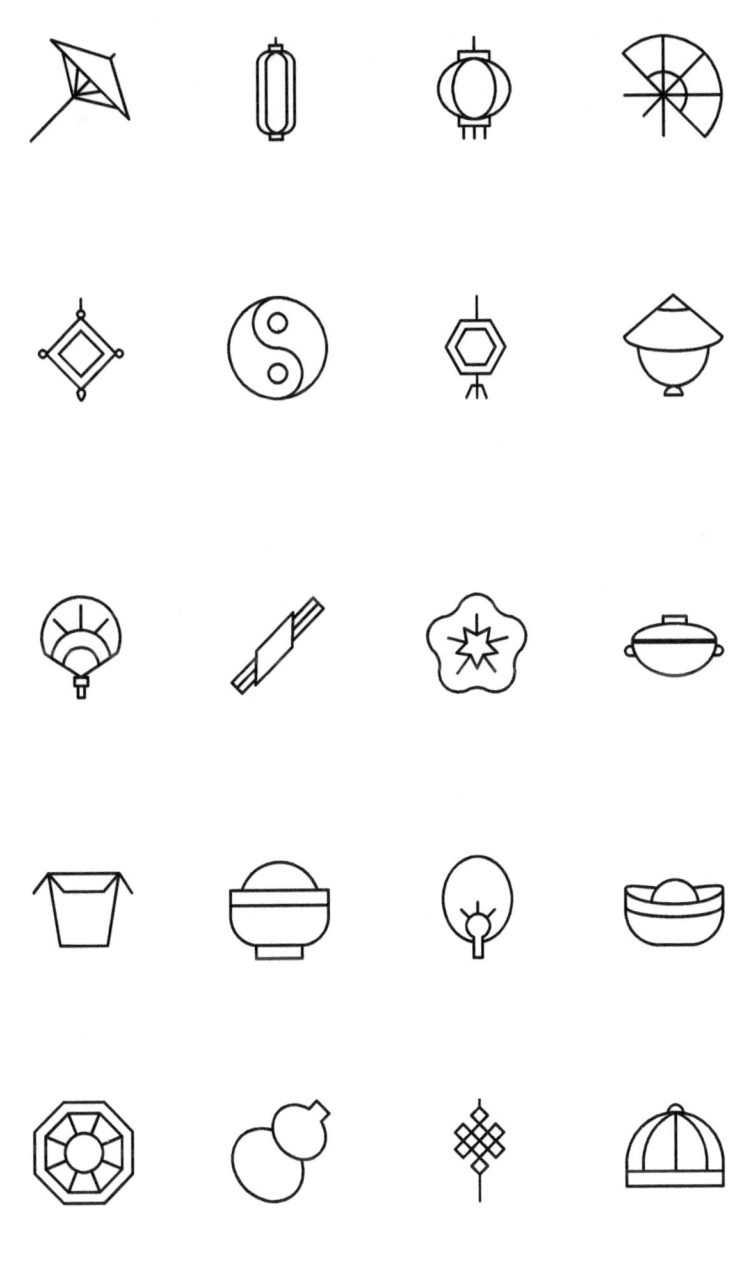

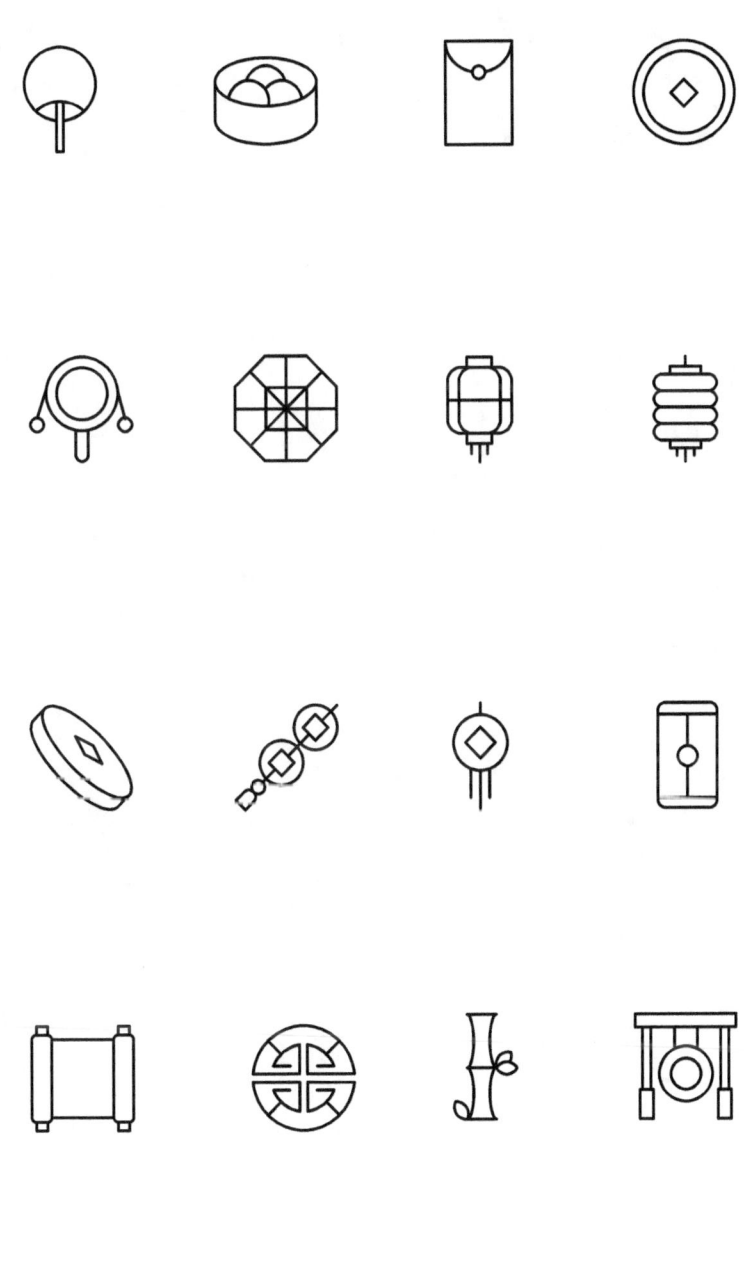

 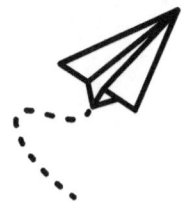 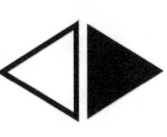
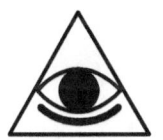  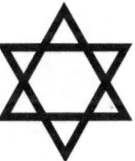
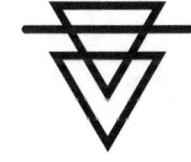  

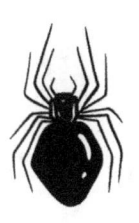
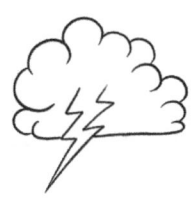
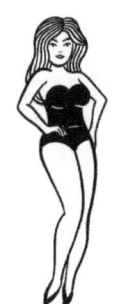
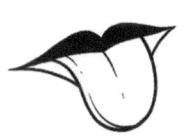
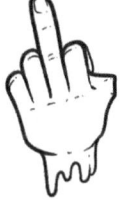
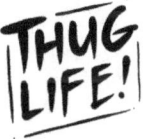
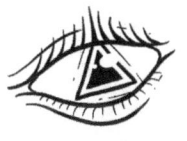
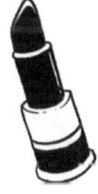
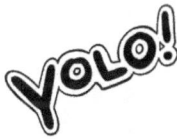
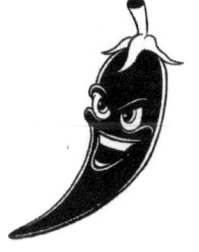
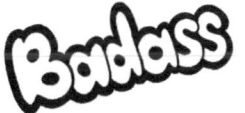
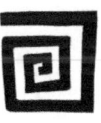

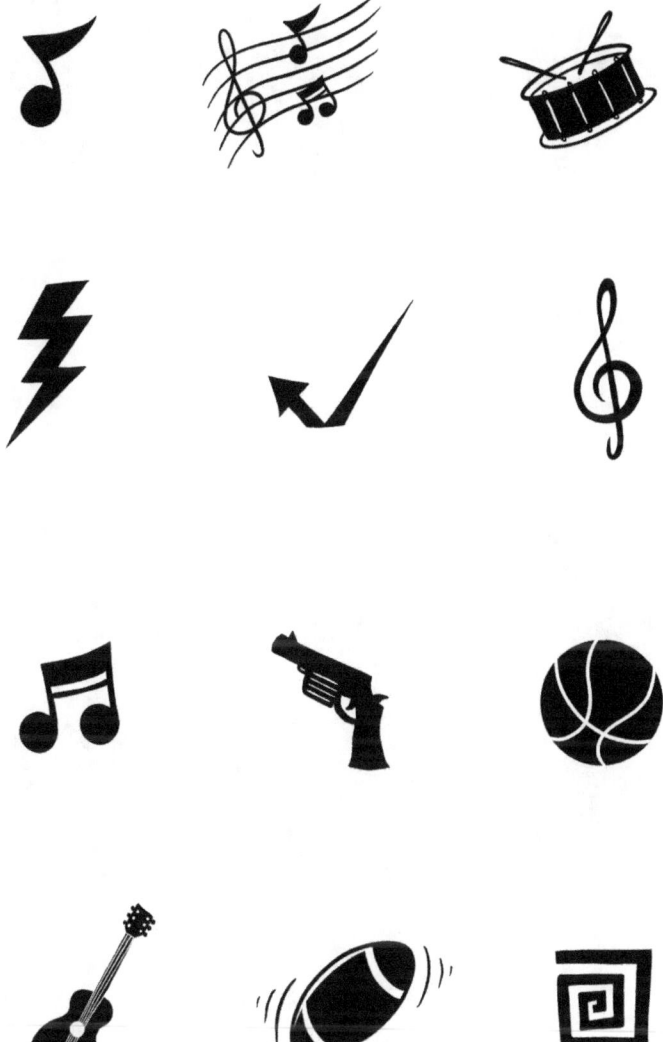

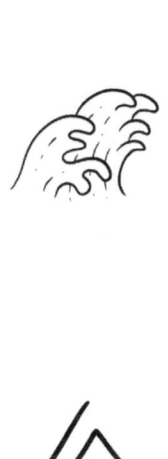
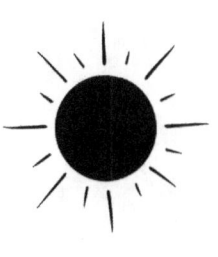

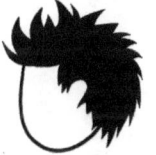
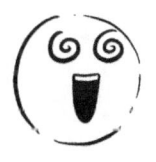

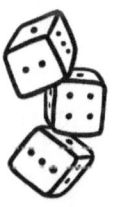
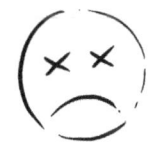
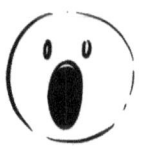
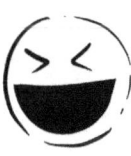

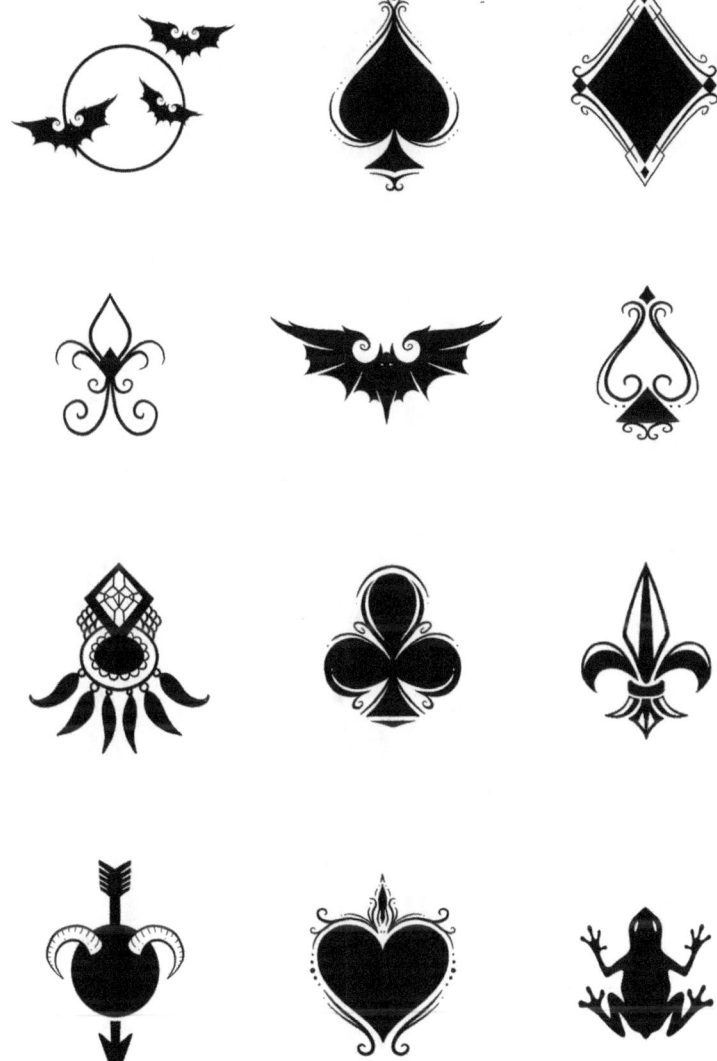

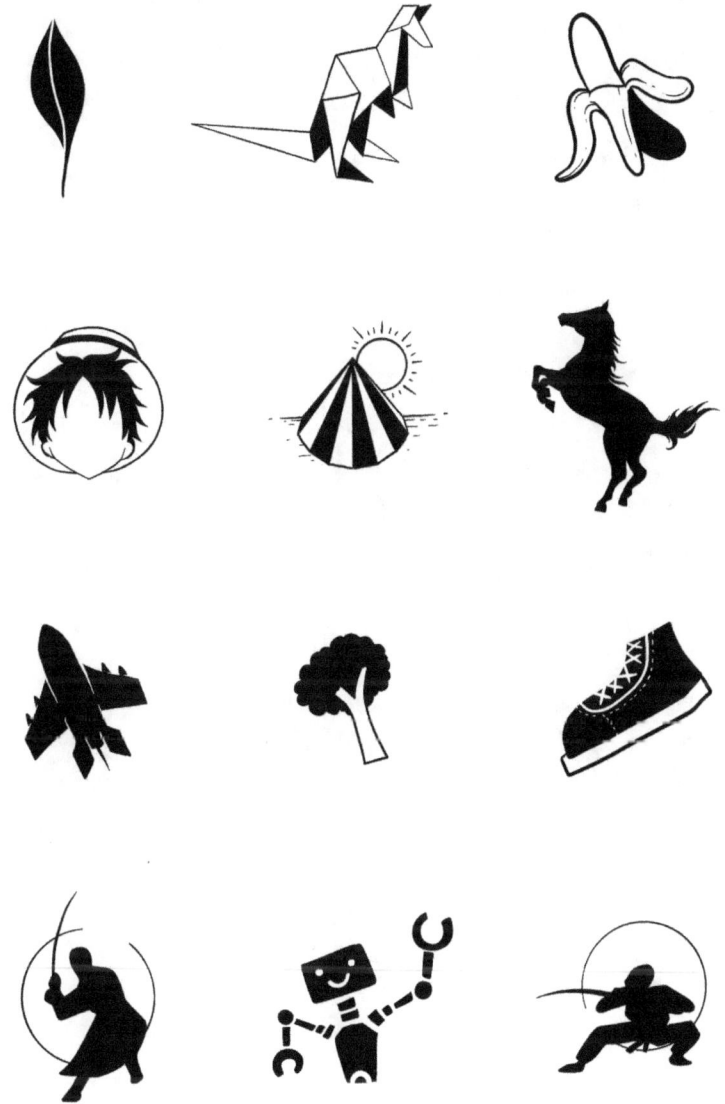

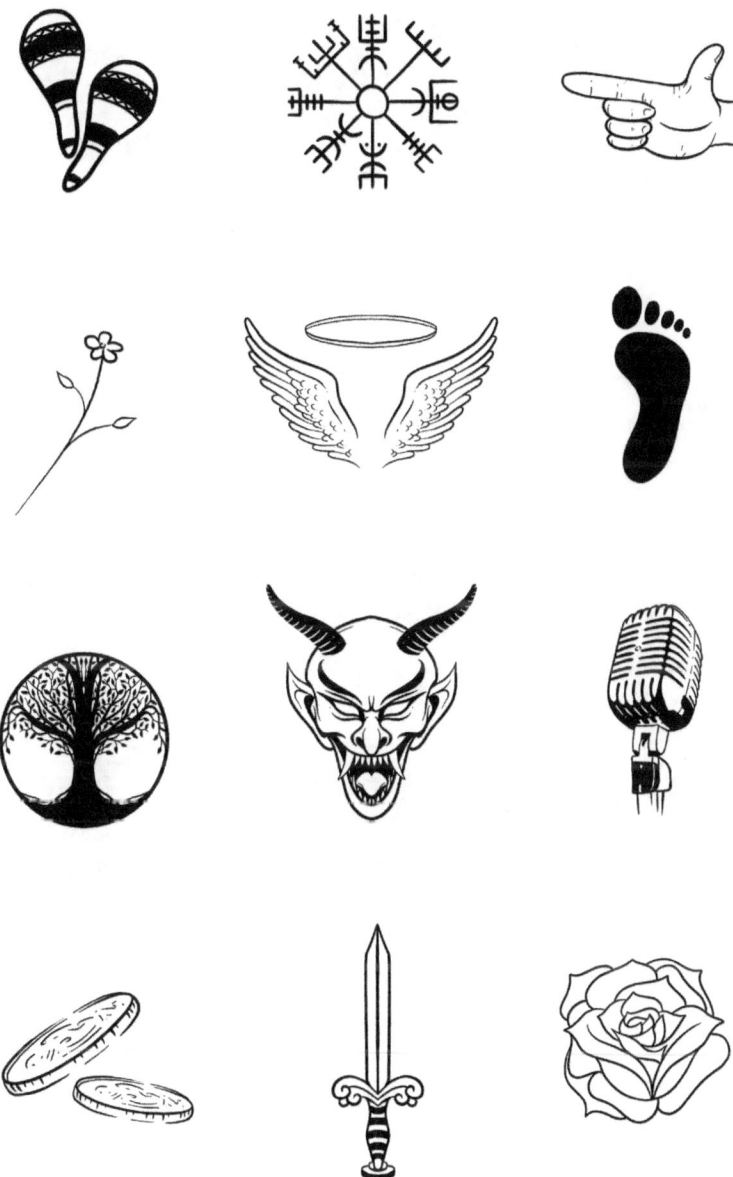

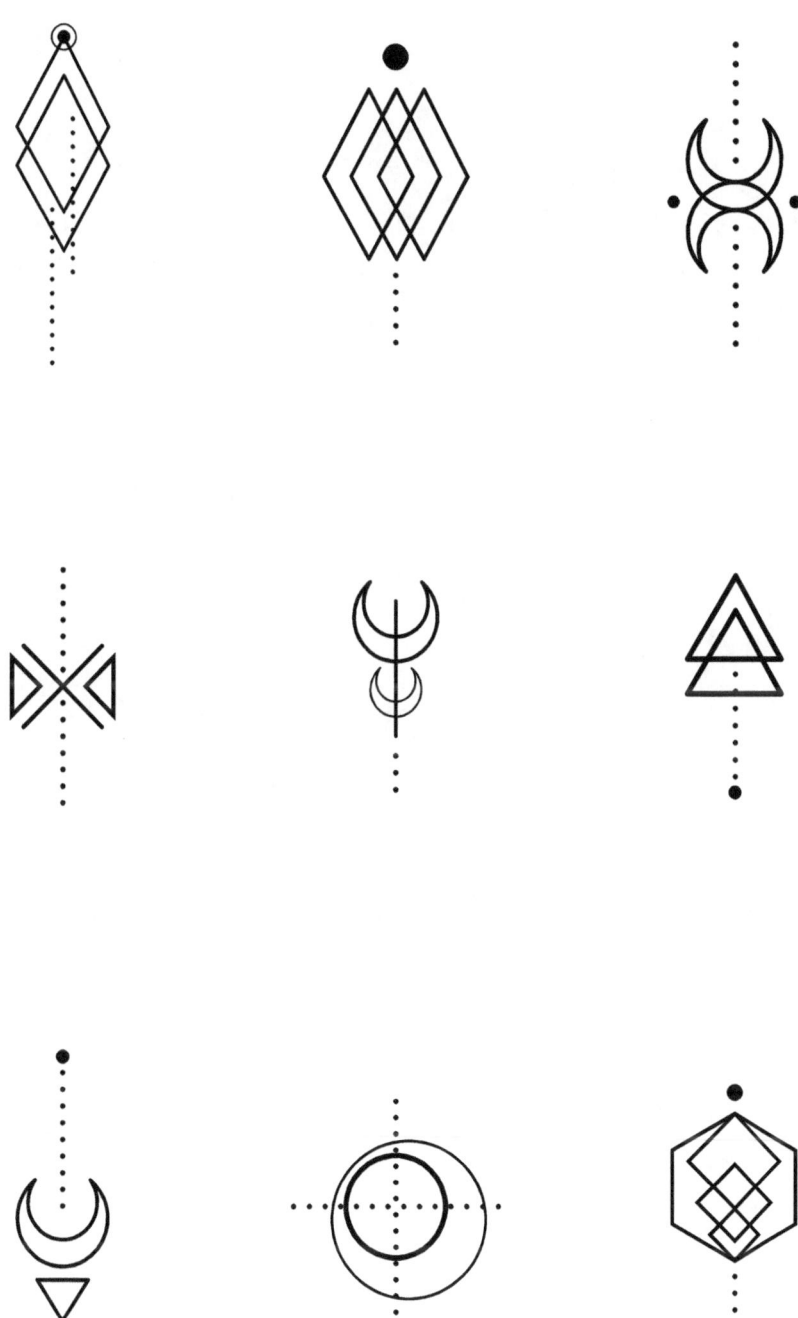

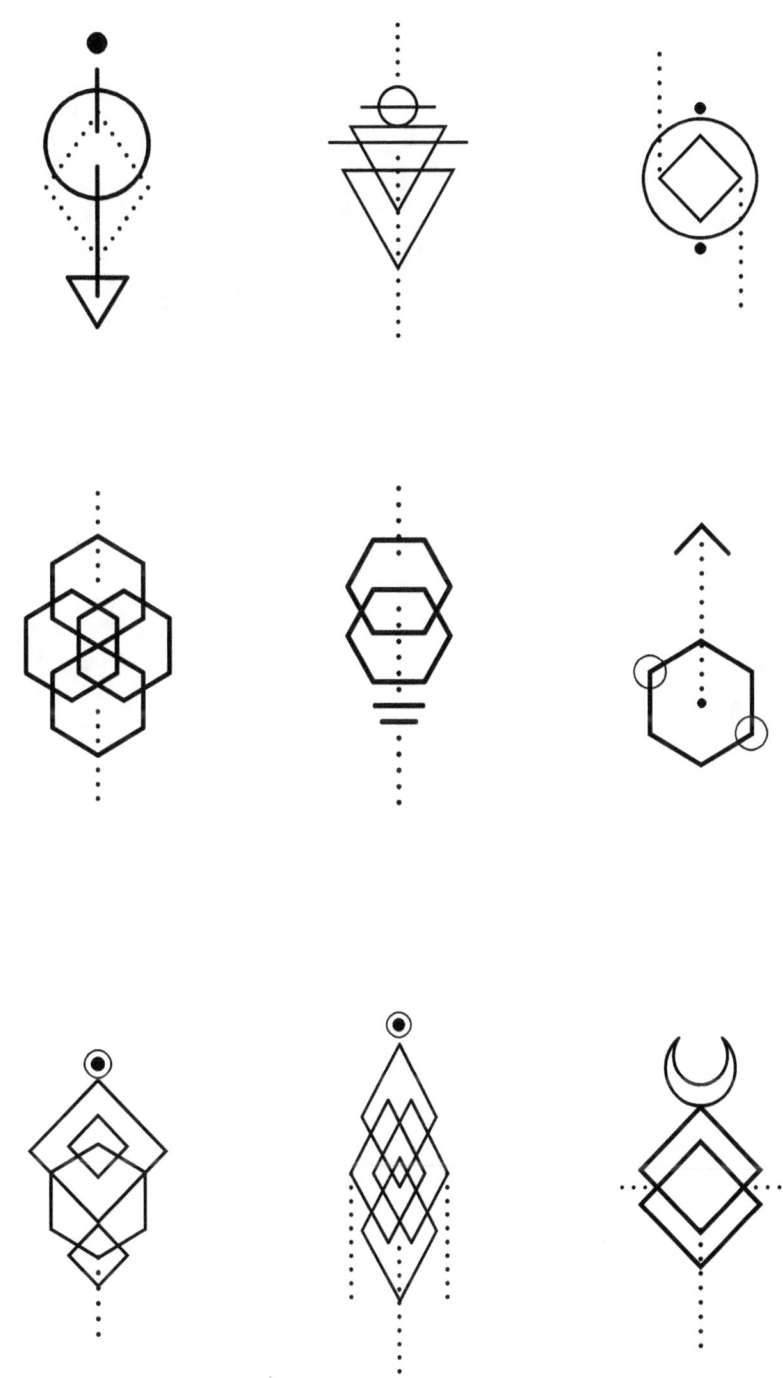

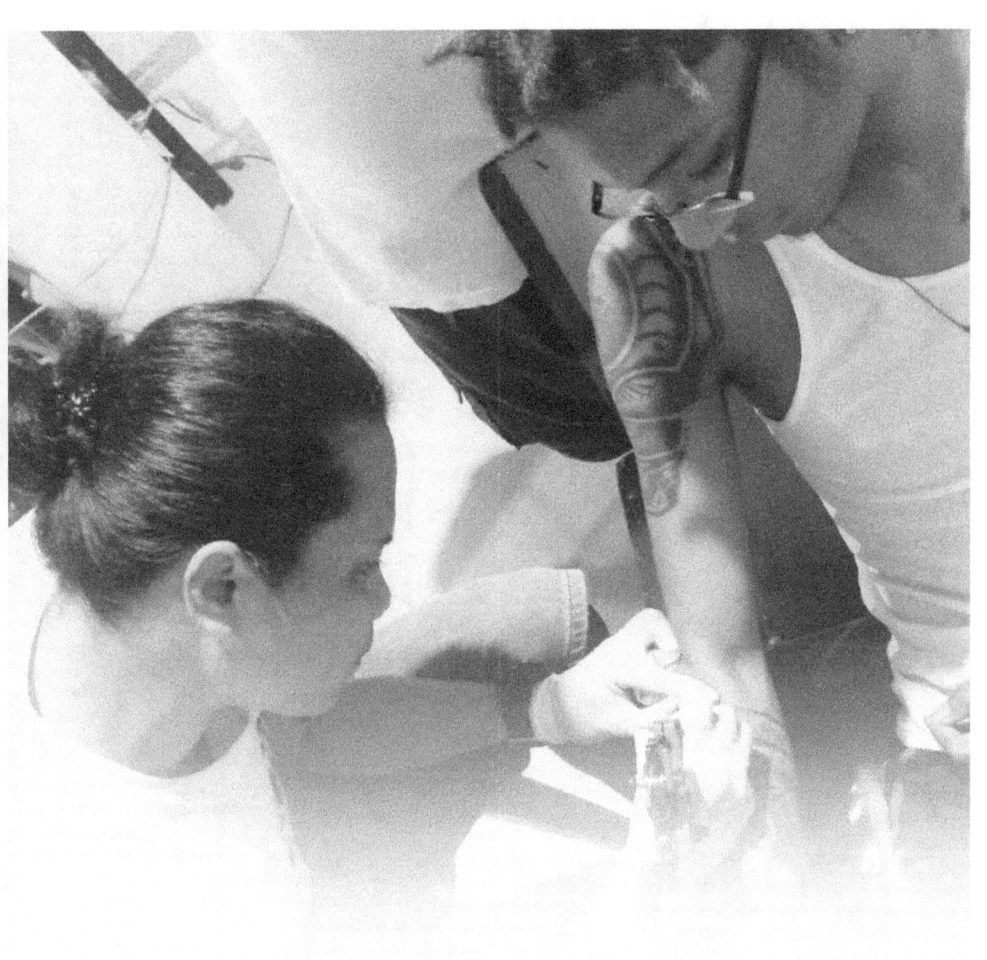

Thank you for your purchase and being our valued customer. We are so grateful for the pleasure of serving you and hope we met your expectations. Your purchase is a big help for me to continue my journey in designing and in the Tattoo industry. - *Diardo Art*

All rights reserved.

No part of this book may be reproduced, distributed or transmitted in any form or by any means, including recording, photocopying, or other electronic methods, without the prior written permission of the publisher.

www.ingramcontent.com/pod-product-compliance
Lightning Source LLC
Chambersburg PA
CBHW070659220526
45466CB00001B/505

A Companion Journal for
Explore, Transform, Flourish:
Support and Hope for Those Who Help Others.

Explore
Transform
Flourish

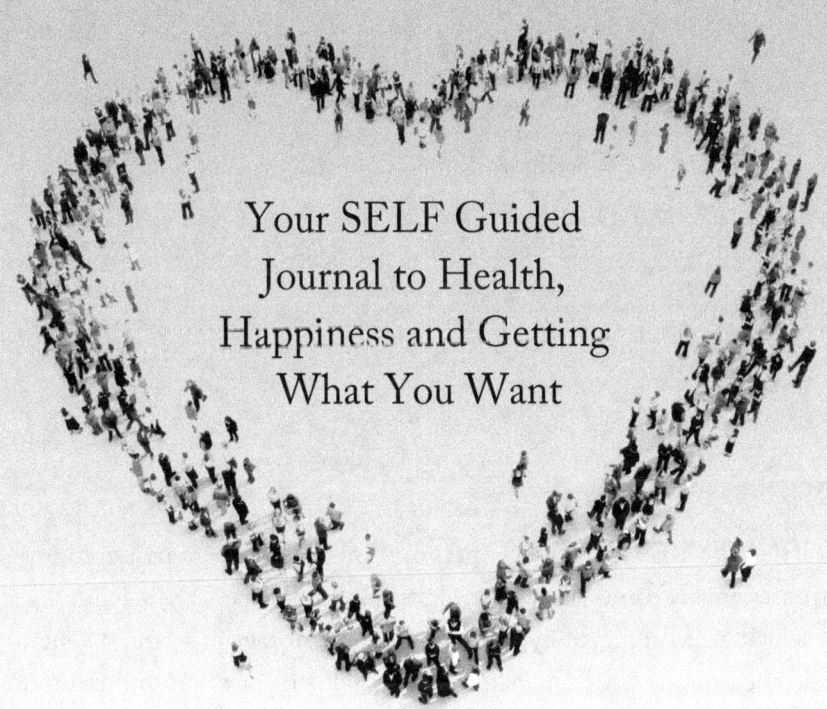

Your SELF Guided
Journal to Health,
Happiness and Getting
What You Want

GILLIAN STEVENS

Copyright © 2020 Gillian Stevens

ALL RIGHTS RESERVED. No part of this book may be reproduced or transmitted in any form whatsoever, electronic, or mechanical, including photocopying, recording, or by any informational storage or retrieval system without the expressed written, dated and signed permission from the author.

Interior formatting by Michael Boalch

Book Cover Design by Black Card Books